HAL LEONARD

VOCAL METHOD

Soprano/Alto Edition

PLAYBACK+

Speed • Pitch • Balance • Loop

To access audio and video visit:
www.halleonard.com/mylibrary

Enter Code
6584-6737-1908-5434

ISBN 978-1-70510-759-1

Visit Hal Leonard Online at
www.halleonard.com

Contact us:
Hal Leonard
7777 West Bluemound Road
Milwaukee, WI 53213
Email: info@halleonard.com

In Europe, contact:
Hal Leonard Europe Limited
42 Wigmore Street
Marylebone, London, W1U 2RN
Email: info@halleonardeurope.com

In Australia, contact:
Hal Leonard Australia Pty. Ltd.
4 Lentara Court
Cheltenham, Victoria, 3192 Australia
Email: info@halleonard.com.au

INTRODUCTION

Congratulations! If you are reading this then you are thinking about becoming a better singer. Our goal is to help you by providing both techniques and songs that will lead you to success.

If you take a moment to think about what makes a singer "popular," you will realize that it's not necessarily about having the "greatest" voice but rather the most "unique" and recognizable instrument AND the ability to tell a good story through song.

Of course, singing in tune and with musicality is a major part of the equation, but the goal here is to further your "unique" instrument and provide positive reinforcement and concepts that will make you more effective and confident when you perform. I guarantee that if you will follow the advice in this book, those goals will be met and your enjoyment of singing enhanced.

Best wishes,
Roger Emerson

HOW TO USE THIS BOOK

The book is divided into two sections: PREPARATION and SONGS. We have included both lyric sheets and notation. If you would like to learn more about notation, please check out "Sight Singing Made Simple" by David Bauguess (HL47819111).

You may be tempted to jump right to the songs, but I encourage you start with the Preparation section. Like a good athlete, warming up and skill exercises are important before you start playing. The same can be said for successful singing!

The songs are generally sequenced with the easiest at the beginning and the more challenging towards the end, but feel free to jump around and sing those songs that motivate you the most, first. A variety of styles have been provided for your enjoyment and growth. The songs are presented in a variety of keys. Some will fit the lower (alto) voice, while others the higher (soprano) voice. Having said that, don't lock yourself into any one vocal classification. The goal should always be to sing the widest range possible. Also, this book features the *PLAYBACK+* feature which allows you to change the key up or down to better fit your comfort range. You can also speed up or slow down the song as desired for practice or performance.

Finally, each song will have suggestions for effective performance provided. Often the suggestion will apply to other songs in the book as well. Remember, these are only ideas. Singing is an art, and you should make the song your own and provide your own treatment. Effective communication of the lyric (telling the story) is the ultimate goal. Let's begin!

POSTURE ▶

As with any "method" book, holding the instrument is a good starting point. Realize that your voice IS a true instrument. It may not have buttons or strings, but it does have all the components of a typical musical instrument, i.e., a method of propulsion (air), a sound generator (the vocal cords) and a resonator (your mouth and face).

EXERCISE 1:

- Stand Tall.

- Feet spaced evenly with your shoulders.

- Strong foot slightly ahead of the other.

- Arms relaxed at your sides.

- Rib cage elevated but not rigid.

As a singer, you most likely will move somewhat when singing, particularly if you are using a hand-held microphone. One hand may hold the mic while the other is used for expression. If the mic is on a stand you may use both hands for expression. Be careful not to overdo motion. It is better to "bring the audience to you," with the face being the primary means of communication.

PHYSICAL WARM-UP ▶

Because we sing with our "entire body," it's a good idea to do a few stretches before we sing.

These are like any physical warmup you would do before an athletic event.

EXERCISE 2:

Do each several times.

- Raise your hands over your head and reach high.

- Wave arms left and right.

- Bring arms down to side and shake them out.

- Roll your shoulders forward, backward, up and down.

- Allow chin to drop to chest and then backward, left and right.

- Hands on hips and rock pelvis forward and back.

- March in place.

- Relax and assume singing posture as described above (stand tall, etc.)

BREATH ▶

Proper breath support and airstream cannot occur effectively if the elements of "posture" outlined above are not employed. Standing tall with the rib cage elevated allows you to breathe fully. It is also important to realize that we sing with our "entire body," from our feet to the top of our head.

If room allows, lie on your back. Begin by exhaling all the air in your lungs then inhale to a slow eight counts (about eight seconds). You may breathe through your nose, mouth or some combination as most singers do. Sense the expansion that occurs around your mid-section. Now exhale for eight counts through pursed lips, as if you are going to whistle but make no sound. This sensation of a "full breath" and controlled exhalation "air stream" are VERY important to successful vocal production. Repeat this exercise four times.

USING THE BREATH

Since air is such an important part of a vibrant vocal sound, don't skimp on these exercises, and make sure that the "sensation" of a full breath and controlled exhalation is a conscious part of "singing" each phrase of every song you sing. **Let me repeat: Remember to take a full breath before every phrase that you sing and then use the air to propel the phrase!**

EXERCISE 3:

- With singing posture in place, breathe in low and deep to a slow eight counts. (Remember the sensation should be the same as when you were lying flat.)

- Now hiss the air out (exhale) for a slow eight counts. (Repeat four times.)

- Breathe in low and deep to a slow 12 counts. Feel the sensation of expansion around your navel and back. DO NOT let shoulders heave up and down. The upper body remains relaxed and the rib cage elevated but not rigid.

- Hiss the air out for a slow 12 counts. Notice how once you have exhaled fully, air will naturally flow back into the lungs. (Repeat 4 times.)

- Breathe in quickly to four counts and do a relaxed sigh from high to low. (Repeat four times.)

PHONATION - MAKING A SOUND

You are now ready to sing! In fact, you just did when you "sighed" from high to low in the last exercise. Singing is nothing more than a "sustained sigh."

Try this: Breathe in (inhale) to a quick 4 count, sigh from high to low but halfway down, hold that pitch and continue the sound until the breath is fully exhaled. If posture is in place, and you've taken a full, low breath, the result should be a full and vibrant sound.

If you are like most people, you probably sighed on an "ah" like a yawn in the morning. That is good and natural. Now try this:

Sigh from high to low with your lips closed to a hum. Midway down, open to an "ah."

Repeat four times.

Let's experiment by stopping at various points from high to low and going from a "hum" to an "ah." Don't forget to inhale fully and let the exhalation do the work! If you find yourself forcing the sound, go back to that "morning sigh."

LET'S USE ALL THAT WE HAVE LEARNED!

If you are not familiar with musical notation, please check out "Sight Singing Made Simple" by David Bauguess (HL47819111).

WARMUP #1

Let's do a variation of the same warmup.

WARMUP #2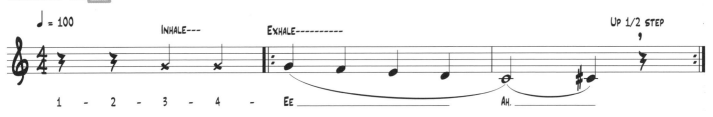

GREAT WORK!

VOWELS

Space inside the mouth will create a richer sounding singing voice. An easy way to "feel" this space is by imagining what you do when you eat something very hot and try not to burn the inside of your mouth.

You have probably heard the term "tall vowels." Simply stated, a "tall vowel" is an ah, oh, oo, ee or eh sound that is sung with the jaw lowered, and the soft pallet at the back of the throat raised (Like you do when you eat something hot!). The lips are also slightly pursed on all but the ah vowel.

If you put your fingers to the jaw hinge adjacent to your ear and open wide, you will feel a space created. Classical singers use VERY tall vowels, the pop singer not so much as popular music does not require nearly as much resonance but it is still important to recognize these five vowel sounds which occur within the lyrics of a song. These vowel shapes can be emphasized on long sounds to make the voice sound better. Let's refer to them as "warm vowels."

Here is an exercise to practice these vowel shapes:

WARMUP #3

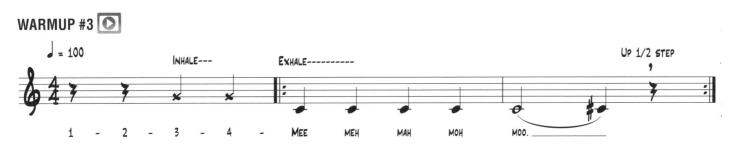

CONSONANTS

Consonants (t, p, m, n, c, etc.) provide clarity and energy to your singing. A simple exercise is to quickly repeat the phrase: "The lips, the teeth, the tip of the tongue!"

WARMUP #4

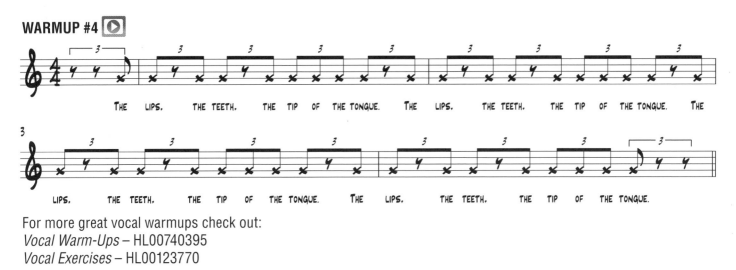

For more great vocal warmups check out:
Vocal Warm-Ups – HL00740395
Vocal Exercises – HL00123770

LET'S SING!

SOMETHING TO TALK ABOUT

FUN FACTS:

"Something to Talk About" was written by Canadian singer-songwriter Shirley Eikhard and recorded by Bonnie Raitt in 1990. Anne Murray wanted to record the song in 1986, but her producers did not think it would be a hit. She still called the album that she released that year "Something to Talk About" even though it did not include the song.

PERFORMANCE TIPS: ▶

As with many country artists, the vocal tone used is brighter. We call that "singing in the mask" as the tone is placed more in the front of the mouth. Also, with this song the short phrases lend themselves to "talking" the notes a bit instead of sustaining them as is more common.

Our voice has many tone colors but most often we refer to them as "dark" or "bright." To practice this, sing an "ah" deep in the back of the throat and gradually move it forward to the front of the teeth then back again. I use a scale of 1 to 10, with 1 being the darkest and 10 the brightest. This song can be sung on about an 8.

EXAMPLE 1:

More songs like this can be found in *Contemporary Hits* Pro Vocal Women's Edition, Volume 3 (HL00740246).

SOMETHING TO TALK ABOUT

Words and Music by Shirley Eikhard

People are talkin', talkin' 'bout people.

I hear them whisper, you won't believe it.

They think we're lovers kept undercover.

I just ignore it, but they keep sayin'

We laugh just a little too loud,

Stand just a little too close,

We stare just a little too long.

Maybe they're seein' somethin' we don't, darlin'.

Let's give 'em somethin' to talk about.

Let's give 'em somethin' to talk about.

Let's give 'em somethin' to talk about.

How about love, love?

I feel so foolish, I never noticed.

You'd act so nervous, could you be fallin' for me?

It took a rumor to make me wonder.

Now I'm convinced I'm goin' under,

Thinkin' 'bout you every day,

Dreamin' 'bout you every night.

I'm hopin' that you feel the same way.

Now that we know it, let's really show it, darlin'.

Let's give 'em somethin' to talk about.

A little myst'ry to figure out.

Let's give 'em somethin' to talk about.

How about love, love, love?

Let's give 'em somethin' to talk about, babe,

A little myst'ry to figure out.

Let's give 'em somethin' to talk about.

How about love?

Ooh, leaves a little, babe. A little myst'ry won't hurt 'em.

Let's give 'em somethin' to talk about.

How about the love, love, love?

Ooh hoo, ooh. Ooh, ooh hoo,

How about love, love, love?

SOMETHING TO TALK ABOUT

Words and Music by
Shirley Eikhard

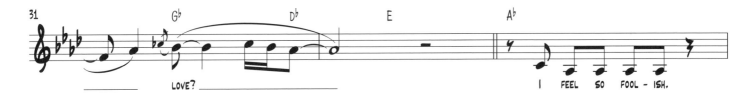

31

LOVE? _____ I FEEL SO FOOL-ISH.

34

I NEV-ER NO-TICED. YOU'D ACT SO NERV-OUS. COULD YOU BE FALL-IN' FOR ME? _

37

_____ IT TOOK A RU-MOR TO MAKE ME WON-DER. _____ NOW _____ I'M CON-VINCED I'M

40

GO - IN' UN - DER. THINK-IN' 'BOUT YOU EV-ER-Y DAY. _____ DREAM-

43

- IN' 'BOUT YOU EV-ER-Y NIGHT. _____ I'M HOP - IN' THAT YOU FEEL THE SAME WAY. _

46

_____ NOW THAT WE KNOW IT. LET'S REAL-LY SHOW IT. DAR-LIN'.

49

LET'S GIVE 'EM SOME-THIN' TO TALK A-BOUT. A LIT-TLE MYS-T'RY TO FIG-

52

URE OUT. _____ LET'S GIVE 'EM SOME-THIN' TO TALK A-BOUT. HOW A-BOUT LOVE. _

55

_____ LOVE. _____ LOVE? _____

LET'S GIVE 'EM SOME-THIN' TO TALK __ A - BOUT. __ BABE. A LIT - TLE MYS - T'RY TO FIG-

URE OUT. __ LET'S GIVE 'EM SOME-THIN' TO TALK A - BOUT. HOW A - BOUT LOVE? __

OOH. __

LEAVES A LIT - TLE, BABE. __ A LIT - TLE MYS - T'RY WON'T HURT 'EM. __

LET'S GIVE 'EM SOME - THIN' TO TALK A - BOUT. HOW A - BOUT THE LOVE. LOVE. __ LOVE? __

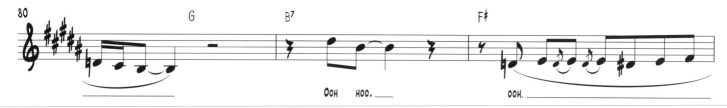

OOH HOO. __ OOH. __

OOH. __ OOH HOO. __

HOW A - BOUT LOVE. __ LOVE. __ LOVE? __

REPEAT AND FADE

AT LAST

FUN FACTS:

"At Last" was written in 1941 for the film musical *Sun Valley Serenade*, but didn't rocket to success until Etta James recorded it 20 years later! Etta James was born Jamesetta Hawkins on January 25, 1938 in Los Angeles. Known for her amazing voice, many people considered James the "Queen of Soul" before Aretha Franklin claimed the title in the 1960s.

PERFORMANCE TIPS: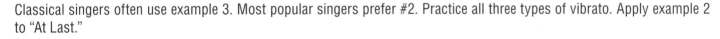

Vibrato is a slightly tremulous effect imparted to vocal or instrumental tone for added warmth and expressiveness by slight and rapid variations in pitch. It is the opposite of straight tone. It can be slow or fast and in popular music is often added at phrase endings to "warm" the sound. Listen and imitate the examples below:

EXAMPLE 1: STRAIGHT TONE

EXAMPLE 2: STRAIGHT TONE TO VIBRATO

EXAMPLE 3: DIRECTLY TO VIBRATO

Classical singers often use example 3. Most popular singers prefer #2. Practice all three types of vibrato. Apply example 2 to "At Last."

(If the key of the recording is too low for your voice, use the *PLAYBACK+* feature to raise the key.)

More songs like this can be found in *Jazz Vocal Standards* Pro Vocal Women's Edition, Volume 18 (HL00740376).

AT LAST

Lyric by Mack Gordon
Music by Harry Warren

At last, my love has come along,

My lonely days are over, and life is like a song.

At last, the skies above are blue.

My heart was wrapped up in clover the night I looked at you.

I found a dream that I could speak to,

A dream that I can call my own.

I found a thrill to press my cheek to,

A thrill that I have never known.

Oh, you smiled, oh, and then the spell was cast.

And here we are in heaven,

For you are mine, at last.

AT LAST

Lyric by Mack Gordon
Music by Harry Warren

The night I _____ looked at you. I found a

dream that I could speak to. _____ A dream that

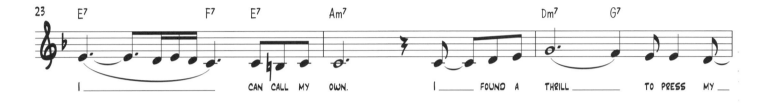

I _____ can call my own. I _____ found a thrill _____ to press my _____

_____ cheek to. a thrill that I _____ have nev-er

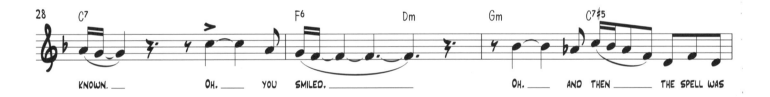

known. _____ Oh, _____ you smiled. _____ Oh, _____ and then _____ the spell was

cast. _____ And here _____ we are _____ in heav-en.

for you are mine. _____ at _____ last. _____

PART OF YOUR WORLD

FUN FACTS:

"Part of Your World" was featured in the Disney animated film *The Little Mermaid.* The late Howard Ashman, who penned the lyrics, strongly believed that the show needed an "I want" song, which is a number during a show in which the main character sings about what they want to accomplish. Disney executive Jeffery Katzenberg wanted it to be about her love interest Eric, however Ashman convinced him that her real desire was her fascination with the "real world."

Katzenberg wanted the song removed from the movie as he thought it would bore children.

PERFORMANCE TIPS: ▶

Communicating the idea of a song is done by emphasizing the lyrics. For a singer to do that, they must enunciate clearly using the consonants of each word and the "articulators," better known as the lips, the teeth, and the tongue. Warmup #4 in part 1 of this book and the exercise below will help you do just that. Keep this clarity in mind when singing the lyrics to "Part of Your World."

EXAMPLE 1:

SIT ON A PO - TA - TO PAN. O - TIS!   SIT ON A PO - TA - TO PAN. O - TIS!*

* A PALINDROME... THE SAME PHRASE FORWARD AND BACKWARD!

More Songs like this can be found in *Disney's Best* Pro Vocal Volume 11 (HL00740344).

PART OF YOUR WORLD

Music by Alan Menken
Lyric by Howard Ashman

Look at this stuff. Isn't it neat?

Wouldn't you think my collection's complete?

Wouldn't you think I'm the girl, the girl who has ev'rything.

Look at this trove, treasures untold.

How many wonders can one cavern hold?

Looking around here you'd think, sure, she's got ev'rything.

I've got gadgets and gizmos a-plenty.

I got whozits and whatzits galore.

You want thingamabobs? I've got twenty,

But who cares? No big deal. I want more.

I wanna be where the people are.

I wanna see, wanna see 'em dancin'.

Walkin' around on those, whatdya call 'em, oh, feet.

Flippin' your fins, you don't get too far.

Legs are required for jumpin', dancin',

Strollin' along down the, what's that word again, street.

Up where they walk, up where they run,

Up where they stay all day in the sun.

Wanderin' free, wish I could be part of that world.

What would I give if I could live out of these waters.

What would I pay to spend a day warm on the sand.

Betcha on land they understand.

Bet they don't reprimand their daughters.

Bright young women, sick of swimmin', ready to stand.

And ready to know what the people know.

Ask 'em my questions and get some answers.

What's a fire, and why does it, what's the word, burn.

When's it my turn? Wouldn't I love, love to explore that shore up above,

Out of the sea. Wish I could be part of that world.

PART OF YOUR WORLD

Music by Alan Menken
Lyrics by Howard Ashman

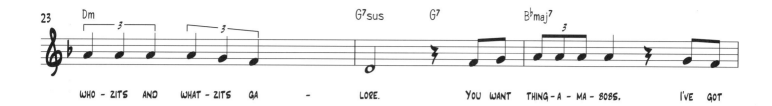

WHO - ZITS AND WHAT - ZITS GA - LORE. YOU WANT THING - A - MA - BOBS, I'VE GOT

TWEN - TY, BUT WHO CARES? NO BIG DEAL. I WANT MORE. ___

___ I WAN - NA BE ___ WHERE THE PEO - PLE ARE.

I WAN - NA SEE, ___ WAN - NA SEE 'EM DANC - IN', WALK - IN' A - ROUND ___ ON THOSE.

WHAT - D' - YA CALL ___ 'EM, OH, FEET.

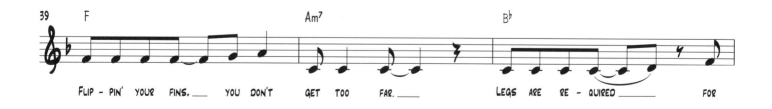

FLIP - PIN' YOUR FINS, ___ YOU DON'T GET TOO FAR. ___ LEGS ARE RE - QUIRED ___ FOR

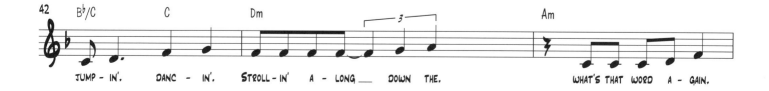

JUMP - IN', DANC - IN', STROLL - IN' A - LONG ___ DOWN THE. WHAT'S THAT WORD A - GAIN.

45 B♭/C   C7   F

STREET?   UP WHERE THEY WALK.   UP WHERE THEY

48 F/E♭   B♭/D   B♭m/D♭

RUN. UP WHERE THEY STAY ALL DAY ____ IN THE SUN. WAN - DER - IN'

51 F/C   B♭/C   C   F   Fmaj7

FREE. WISH I COULD BE PART OF THAT WORLD. ____ WHAT WOULD I

55 B♭   C/B♭   Am   Dm   Dm/C

GIVE IF I COULD LIVE OUT - TA THESE WA - TERS? WHAT WOULD I

59 B♭   C/B♭   Am   F9sus   F

PAY TO SPEND A DAY WARM ON THE SAND? BET - CHA ON

63 B♭   C/B♭   A7sus   A7

LAND THEY UN - DER - STAND. BET THEY DON'T RE - PRI - MAND ____ THEIR DAUGH -

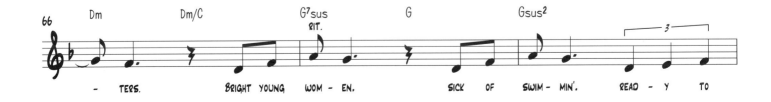

66 Dm   Dm/C   G7sus   G   Gsus2
                       RIT.

- TERS. BRIGHT YOUNG WOM - EN. SICK OF SWIM - MIN'. READ - Y TO

STAND. _____ AND READ - Y TO KNOW ____ WHAT THE

PEO - PLE KNOW. ASK 'EM MY QUES - TIONS AND GET SOME AN - SWERS.

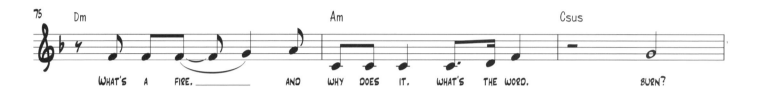

WHAT'S A FIRE, _____ AND WHY DOES IT, WHAT'S THE WORD, BURN?

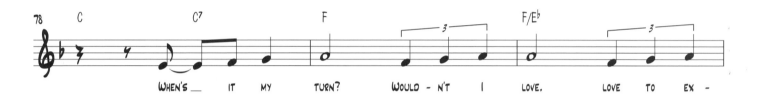

WHEN'S ___ IT MY TURN? WOULD - N'T I LOVE, LOVE TO EX -

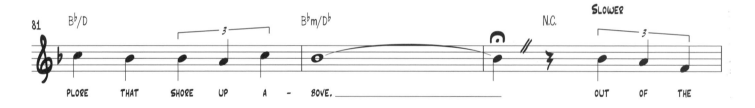

PLORE THAT SHORE UP A - BOVE, _____ OUT OF THE

SEA. WISH I COULD BE

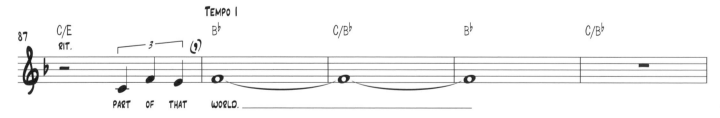

PART OF THAT WORLD. _____

BYE, BYE, BLACKBIRD

FUN FACTS:

"Bye, Bye, Blackbird" was written in 1926 and has become a "standard" (part of the country's well-known music literature). As was common in songs of that era, there was a verse that preceded and set up the chorus that today we know as the entire song (the verse has been omitted). Many songs including "White Christmas" had a verse that few people are aware of, and this verse is seldom sung as well.

PERFORMANCE TIPS:

A hallmark of songs performed in a "swing" style is that they are sung "conversationally" and relaxed. And when we say a song "swings" what it really means is that the eighth notes are treated unevenly as part of a triplet instead of evenly (straight) as you would find in most pop, rock and Latin songs. Listen to the two examples below which demonstrate the difference.

EXAMPLE 1: STRAIGHT

EXAMPLE 2: WITH A SWING AND CONVERSATIONAL

More songs like this can be found in *Jazz Standards* Pro Vocal Volume 2 (HL00740249).

BYE, BYE BLACKBIRD

Lyric by Mort Dixon
Music by Ray Henderson

Pack up all my care and woe,

Here I go singing low.

Bye, bye blackbird.

When somebody waits for me,

Sugar's sweet, so is he.

Bye, bye blackbird.

No one here could love and understand me.

Oh, what hard luck stories they all hand me.

Make my bed and light the light,

I'll arrive a late tonight.

Blackbird, bye, bye.

No one here could love and understand me.

Oh, what hard luck stories they all hand me.

Make my bed and light the light,

I'll arrive a late tonight.

Blackbird, blackbird, blackbird bye, bye.

BYE, BYE BLACKBIRD

Lyric by Mort Dixon
Music by Ray Henderson

ROLLING IN THE DEEP

FUN FACT:

"Rolling In The Deep" was the first single released on Adele's second album, *21*. Her albums are numbered, the first being *19*, by the age she was when the album was recorded.

PERFORMANCE TIPS:

Whenever multiple notes are sung on one word it is called a melisma. To effectively sing a melisma, small amounts of breath accents, powered by abdominal muscles are required.

Use the exercise below to build those muscles.

EXAMPLE 1:

More songs like this can be found in *Adele* Pro Vocal Volume 56, 2nd Edition (HL00160119).

ROLLING IN THE DEEP

Words and Music by Adele Adkins and Paul Epworth

There's a fire startin' in my heart,

Reachin' a fever pitch, and it's bringin' me out the dark.

Finally, I can see you crystal clear.

Go ahead and sell me out, and I'll lay your sh*t bare.

See how I'll leave with ev'ry piece of you,

Don't underestimate the things that I will do.

There's a fire starting in my heart,

Reaching a fever pitch, and it's bringin' me out the dark.

The scars of your love remind me of us,

They keep me thinkin' that we almost had it all.

The scars of your love, they leave me breathless.

I can't help feeling

We could've had it all, rollin' in the deep.

You had my heart inside your hand,

And you played it to the beat.

Baby, I have no story to be told,

But I've heard one of you, and I'm gonna make your head burn.

Think of me in the depths of your despair,

Making a home down there, as mine sure won't be shared.

The scars of your love remind me of us,

They keep me thinkin' that we almost had it all.

The scars of your love, they leave me breathless.

I can't help feeling

We could've had it all, rollin' in the deep.

You had my heart inside your hand,

And you played it to the beat.

Could've had it all, rollin' in the deep.

You had my heart inside your hand,

But you played it with a beating.

Throw your soul through every open door,

Count your blessings to find what you look for.

Turn my sorrow into treasured gold,

You'll pay me back in kind, and reap just what you sow.

We could've had it all, we could've had it all, it all, it all, it all.

We could've had it all, rollin' in the deep.

You had my heart inside your hand,

And you played it to the beat.

Could've had it it all, rollin' in the deep.

You had my heart inside your hand,

And you played it, you played it, you played it to the beat.

ROLLING IN THE DEEP

Words and Music by Adele Adkins
and Paul Epworth

There's a ___ fire ___ start-ing in my ___ heart.

Reach-ing ___ a fe-ver pitch, and it's bring-in' me out the dark. ___

The scars of your ___ love re-mind me of ___ us, they keep me

think-in' that we al-most had it all. The scars of your ___ love, they leave me

breath-less. I can't help feel-ing we could-'ve had it all. ___

___ roll-in' in the deep. ___ You had my heart in-

side your hand. ___ and you played ___ it to the beat. ___

___ ba-by, ___ I ___ have no sto-ry to be told. but

37 B♭5   G5   B♭5

I'VE HEARD _____ ONE OF YOU, AND I'M GON-NA MAKE YOUR HEAD BURN.

39 C5   G5

THINK OF _____ ME _____ IN THE DEPTHS OF YOUR DE - SPAIR.

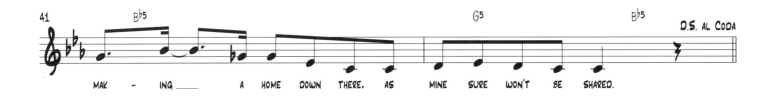

41 B♭5   G5   B♭5   D.S. AL CODA

MAK - ING _____ A HOME DOWN THERE. AS MINE SURE WON'T BE SHARED.

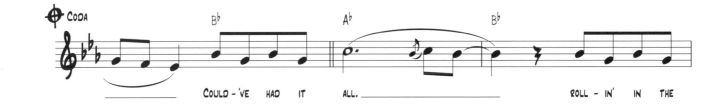

⊕ CODA   B♭   A♭   B♭

_____ COULD - 'VE HAD IT ALL. _____ ROLL - IN' IN THE

46 Cm   B♭   A♭

DEEP. _____ YOU HAD MY HEART IN - SIDE YOUR HAND. _____

49   B♭

_____ BUT YOU PLAYED _____ IT WITH A BEAT - ING.

52 N.C.   3

THROW YOUR _ SOUL _____ THROUGH EV - ER - Y O - PEN DOOR. COUNT YOUR _ BLESS - INGS TO

55   C5

FIND WHAT YOU LOOK FOR. TURN MY _ SOR - ROW IN - TO TREAS-URED GOLD. YOU'LL

PAY ME ___ BACK IN KIND, AND REAP JUST WHAT YOU SOW. ___

WE COULD-'VE HAD IT ALL. ___ WE COULD-'VE HAD IT

ALL, ___ IT ALL, ___ IT ALL, ___ IT ALL. ___

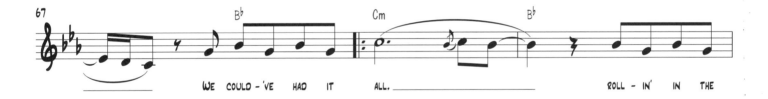

WE COULD-'VE HAD IT ALL, ___ ROLL-IN' IN THE

DEEP. ___ YOU HAD MY HEART IN-SIDE YOUR HAND. ___

{AND BUT} YOU PLAYED ___ IT TO THE BEAT. ___ COULD-'VE HAD IT

___ IT, YOU PLAYED ___ IT, YOU PLAYED ___ IT, YOU PLAYED ___ IT TO THE BEAT. ___

FIELDS OF GOLD

FUN FACTS:

Fields of Gold was written by G.M. Sumner, better known as "Sting." Few people also know that he was an English major and taught English for a while before making it in the music business. Sting's version has a rock beat; however, this setting is fashioned after the ballad version of Eva Cassidy.

PERFORMANCE TIPS:

There are many ways to phrase a line in any song. The cardinal rule however is DO NOT run out of air and take a breath before the last word! It's a common mistake. Below are two examples of the proper way to phrase the first line of "Fields of Gold." The general rule is to sing the complete thought on one breath; however, two shorter phrases can also work well. Note there is a rise and fall to the phrase indicated by a crescendo (get louder) and decrescendo (get softer) hairpin on each phrase.

Also, remember to shape a "warm vowel" on words such as "moves" and "gold."

EXAMPLE 1:

EXAMPLE 2:

FIELDS OF GOLD

Music and Lyrics by Sting

You'll remember me when the west wind moves

Upon the fields of barley.

You'll forget the sun in his jealous sky

As we walk in fields of gold.

So she took her love for to gaze awhile

Upon the fields of barley.

In his arms she fell as her hair came down

Among the fields of gold.

Will you stay with me, will you be my love

Among the fields of barley?

We'll forget the sun in his jealous sky

As we lie in fields of gold.

I never made promises lightly,

And there have been some that I've broken,

But I swear in the days still left

We'll walk in fields of gold.

We will walk in fields of gold.

Many years have passed since those summer days

Among the fields of barley.

See the children run as the sun goes down

Among the fields of gold.

I never made promises lightly,

And there have been some that I've broken,

But I swear in the days still left

We'll walk in fields of gold.

We will walk in fields of gold.

You'll remember me when the west wind moves

Upon the fields of barley.

You can tell the sun in his jealous sky

When we walk in fields of gold.

When we walked in fields of gold.

FIELDS OF GOLD

Music and Lyrics by
Sting

DON'T KNOW WHY

FUN FACTS:

Norah Jones' hit, "Don't Know Why," was re-recorded several times but the producers could never quite equal the vibe of the original demo recording. For that reason, the demo recording is the one that was eventually released and is the one heard around the world today.

PERFORMANCE TIPS: ▶

A moderate ballad like this one needs a smooth, connected, and legato feeling to the vocal. Looking at the complexity of the rhythms on the leadsheet can be misleading. It must be sung in a relaxed way and appear to "float" over the rhythm section. Practice example 1 below using the neutral vowel "oo" then sing the lyric with the same smooth and relaxed quality, example 2.

EXAMPLE 1:

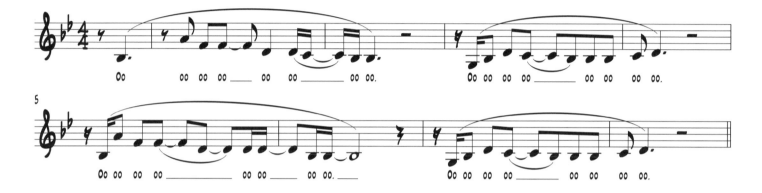

EXAMPLE 2:

More songs like this can be found in *Contemporary Hits* Pro Vocal Women's Edition, Volume 3 (HL00740246)

DON'T KNOW WHY

Words and Music
By Jesse Harris

I waited till I saw the sun.

I don't know why I didn't come.

I left you by the house of fun.

I don't know why I didn't come,

I don't know why I didn't come.

When I saw the break of day,

I wished that I could fly away

'stead of kneeling in the sand

Catching teardrops in my hand.

My heart is drenched in wine,

But you'll be on my mind forever.

Out across the endless sea,

I would die in ecstasy.

But I'll be a bag of bones

Driving down the road alone.

My heart is drenched in wine,

But you'll be on my mind forever.

Something has to make you run.

I don't know why I didn't come.

I feel as empty as a drum.

I don't know why I didn't come,

I don't know why I didn't come,

I don't know why I didn't come.

DON'T KNOW WHY

Words and Music by
Jesse Harris

27 Gm7 / C7 / F7 F7/E♭ B♭/D F/C

YOU'LL BE ON MY MIND FOR - EV - ER.

31 B♭maj7 B♭7 E♭maj7 D+ Gm7 / C7 / F7sus B♭

OUT A - CROSS THE END - LESS SEA. I WOULD DIE IN EC - STA - SY.

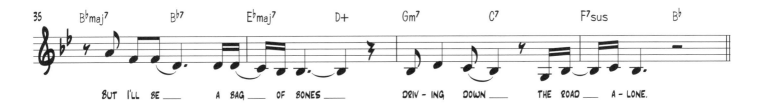

35 B♭maj7 B♭7 E♭maj7 D+ Gm7 / C7 / F7sus B♭

BUT I'LL BE A BAG OF BONES DRIV - ING DOWN THE ROAD A - LONE.

39 Gm7 / C7 / F7

MY HEART IS DRENCHED IN WINE, BUT

43 Gm7 / C7 / F7

YOU'LL BE ON MY MIND FOR - EV - ER.

47 B♭maj7 B♭7 E♭maj7 D7♯5 Gm7 / C7 / F7sus

51 B♭maj7 B♭7 E♭maj7 D+ Gm7 / C7 / F7sus

55 B♭maj7 B♭7 E♭maj7 D+ Gm7 / C7 /

SOME - THING HAS TO MAKE YOU RUN. I DON'T KNOW WHY I DID -

I feel as empty as a drum. I don't know why I didn't come. I don't know why I didn't come. I don't know why I didn't come.

BEAUTY AND THE BEAST

FUN FACTS:

Walt Disney attempted to make *Beauty and the Beast* in the 1930s, but the project never materialized until 1991, long after his passing. It was originally going to be a movie without any music, but after the success of *Little Mermaid*, studio chief Jeffery Katzenberg insisted that it be a musical.

PERFORMANCE TIPS: ▶

It is important to remember that long sounds on the vowels *i* and *a* must be carefully sung as they constitute a double vowel called a *diphthong*. If you sing the 2nd part of a double vowel quickly, your sound will be squeezed and unpleasant. The words *time*, *same,* and *surprise* all contain double vowels, (ah-ee and eh-ee). When these occur sing the open *ah* or *eh* and then close to the *ee* at the very end of the word. Listen to the correct and the incorrect way to sing the first line of "Beauty and the Beast."

EXAMPLE 1: CORRECT

EXAMPLE 2: INCORRECT

More Songs like this can be found in *Disney's Best* Pro Vocal Volume 11 (HL00740344).

BEAUTY AND THE BEAST

Music by Alan Menken

Lyrics by Howard Ashman

Tale as old as time, true as it can be.

Barely even friends, then somebody bends unexpectedly.

Just a little change. Small, to say the least.

Both a little scared, neither one prepared. Beauty and the Beast.

Ever just the same. Ever a surprise.

Ever as before, ever just as sure as the sun will rise.

Tale as old as time. Tune as old as song.

Bittersweet and strange, finding you can change, learning you were wrong.

Certain as the sun rising in the East.

Tale as old as time, song as old as rhyme. Beauty and the Beast.

Tale as old as time, song as old as rhyme. Beauty and the Beast.

BEAUTY AND THE BEAST

Music by Alan Menken
Lyrics by Howard Ashman

A THOUSAND YEARS

FUN FACT:

"A Thousand Years" is considered a "sleeper hit." It was featured in the motion picture *The Twilight Saga: Breaking Dawn – Part 1*, and it suddenly jumped to the top of the charts, becoming Christina Perri's number one single.

PERFORMANCE TIPS: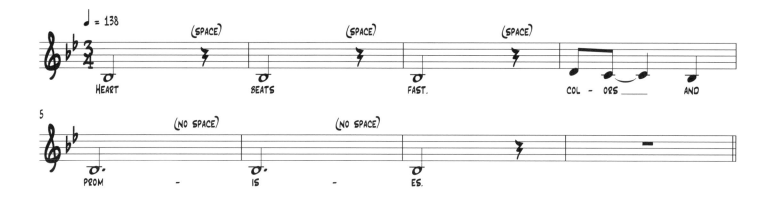

The importance of "silence" when singing cannot be over-emphasized. It is the rests that give music its definition. The first three measures of "A Thousand Years" are excellent examples of the effectiveness of "space" in a vocal line. Make sure that there is complete silence on beat 3 of those measures, in contrast with measures 5 and 6, which contain no rest or space. Also notice the 3/4 time signature at the beginning. It notates a completely different "feel" than does a 4/4 time signature.

EXAMPLE 1:

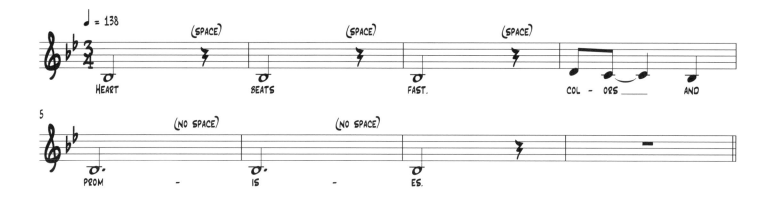

More songs like this can be found in *Top Downloads* Pro Vocal Volume 62 (HL000123120).

A THOUSAND YEARS

Words and music by David Hodges and Christina Perri

Heart beats fast, colors and promises.

How to be brave,

How can I love when I'm afraid to fall?

But watching you stand alone,

All of my doubt suddenly goes away somehow.

One step closer.

I have died ev'ry day, waiting for you.

Darlin', don't be afraid, I have loved you

For a thousand years.

I'll love you for a thousand more.

Time stands still, beauty in all she is.

I will be brave,

I will not let anything take away

what's standing in front of me.

Every breath, every hour has come to this.

One step closer.

I have died ev'ry day, waiting for you.

Darlin', don't be afraid, I have loved you

For a thousand years.

I'll love you for a thousand more.

And all along I believed I would find you.

Time has brought your heart to me. I have loved you

For a thousand years.

I'll love you for a thousand more.

One step closer. One step closer.

I have died ev'ry day, waiting for you.

Darlin', don't be afraid, I have loved you

For a thousand years.

I'll love you for a thousand more.

And all along I believed I would find you.

Time has brought your heart to me. I have loved you

For a thousand years.

I'll love you for a thousand more.

A THOUSAND YEARS

Words and Music by David Hodges
and Christina Perri

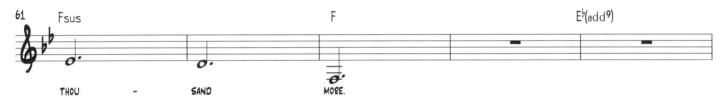

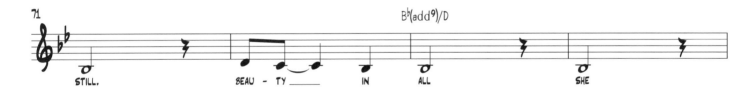

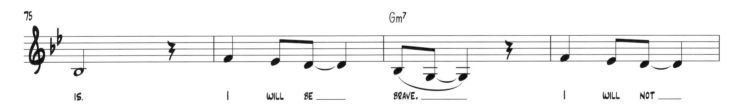

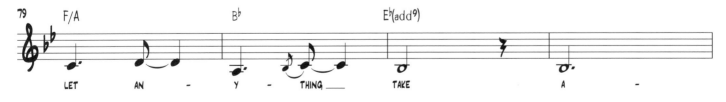

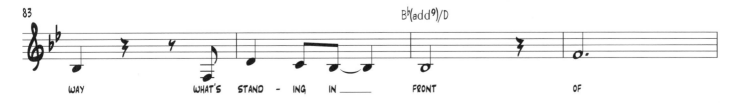

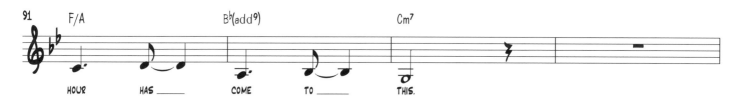

124 B♭/F   E♭

YOU FOR A THOU - SAND YEARS. _____ I'LL

128   Fsus   F

LOVE YOU _____ FOR _____ A THOU - SAND MORE. _____

132   B♭(add⁹)   **13**

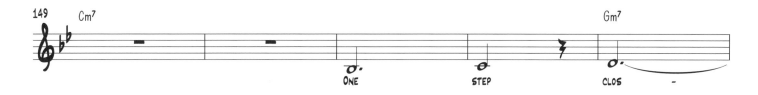

149 Cm⁷   Gm⁷

ONE STEP CLOS -

154   F   Cm⁷

- ER. ONE

160 F   Gm⁷   F/A

STEP CLOS - ER.

165 B♭

I HAVE DIED _____ EV - 'RY DAY, _____ WAIT - ING FOR _____

168 F/A   Gm⁷

_____ YOU. DAR - LIN', DON'T _____ BE A - FRAID. _____ I HAVE LOVED _____

172 B♭/F   E♭(add⁹)

_____ YOU FOR A THOU - SAND YEARS. _____ I'LL

LOVE YOU ____ FOR ____ A THOU - SAND MORE. AND

ALL A - LONG ____ I BE - LIEVED ____ I WOULD FIND _____ YOU.

TIME HAS BROUGHT ____ YOUR HEART TO ME. _____ I HAVE LOVED _____ YOU FOR A

THOU - SAND YEARS. _____ I'LL LOVE YOU ____ FOR ____ A

THOU - SAND MORE.

MAKE YOU FEEL MY LOVE

FUN FACTS:

Written by Bob Dylan in 1997, it was first released commercially by Billy Joel under the title "To Make You Feel My Love." Many other artists have covered this song, most recently, Adele, who, like the others, dropped "To" from the official title.

PERFORMANCE TIPS:

Mature singers have basically 3 registers: chest (low notes), middle (mid-range notes), and head register (high notes). A great deal of pop music is sung in the chest and middle "registers." The goal is to make them all sound smooth and consistent. The bridge on "Make You Feel My Love" (measures 25-32 and 49-56) requires you to go from the chest register to the upper middle register. Use the exercise below to help train your voice to make a smooth transition.

EXERCISE 1:

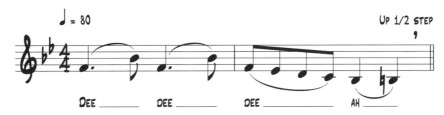

More songs like this can be found in *Adele* Pro Vocal Volume 56, 2nd Edition (HL00160119).

MAKE YOU FEEL MY LOVE

Words and Music by Bob Dylan

When the rain is blowin' in your face

And the whole world is on your case,

I could offer you a warm embrace

To make you feel my love.

When the evenin' shadows and the stars appear

And there is no one there to dry your tears,

I could hold you for a million years

To make you feel my love.

I know you haven't made your mind up yet,

But I would never do you wrong.

I've known it from the moment that we met,

No doubt in my mind where you belong.

I'd go hungry, I'd go black and blue.

I'd go crawlin' down the avenue.

No, there's nothing that I wouldn't do

To make you feel my love.

The storms are raging on the rollin' sea

And on the highway of regret.

The winds of change are blowin' wild and free.

You ain't seen nothin' like me yet.

I could make you happy, make your dreams come true.

Nothing that I, I wouldn't do.

Go to the ends of the earth for you

To make you feel my love,

To make you feel my love.

MAKE YOU FEEL MY LOVE

Words and Music by
Bob Dylan

MIL - LION YEARS _____ TO MAKE YOU FEEL MY _____ LOVE. _____

I KNOW YOU HAVE - N'T MADE YOUR MIND UP YET. ___ BUT I WOULD NEV - ER DO _____ YOU WRONG. ___

I'VE KNOWN IT FROM THE MO - MENT _____ THAT WE _____ MET.

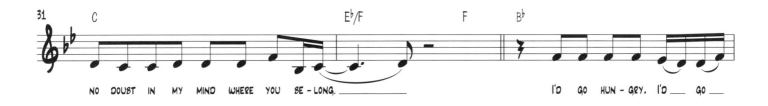

NO DOUBT IN MY MIND WHERE YOU BE - LONG. _____ I'D GO HUN - GRY. I'D _____ GO

BLACK AND BLUE. _____ I'D GO CRAWL - IN' DOWN THE AV - E - NUE. _____

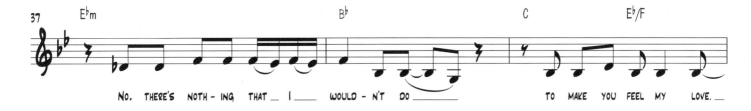

NO. THERE'S NOTH - ING THAT __ I _____ WOULD - N'T DO _____ TO MAKE YOU FEEL MY _____ LOVE. _____

I WILL REMEMBER YOU

FUN FACTS:

"I Will Remember You" is a song written Sarah McLachlan, Seamus Egan, and Dave Merenda. The original inspiration came from Seamus Egan's instrumental song, "Weep Not for the Memories," which appeared on his album *A Week in January* (1990). McLachlan and Merenda added lyrics and modified the melody for her version.

PERFORMANCE TIPS: ▶

Singing ballads is an excellent opportunity to explore phrasing. Phrasing is simply a musical sentence, but the way you perform it makes it exciting or dull. An easy way to add motion and excitement is to simply emphasize important words in each phrase. Listen to the three examples below. There is no correct or incorrect way, but as you learn new songs, underline important words, and give them more emphasis.

EXAMPLE 1:

EXAMPLE 2:

EXAMPLE 3:

An additional resource on phrasing and effective performance is *Singing with Expression* by Rosana Eckert (HL00234967).

More songs like this can be found in *Contemporary Hits* Pro Vocal Women's Edition, Volume 3 (HL00740246).

I WILL REMEMBER YOU

Words and Music by Sarah McLachlan,
Seamus Egan and Dave Merenda

I will remember you.

Will you remember me?

Don't let your life pass you by.

Weep not for the memories.

Remember the good times that we had.

I let them slip away from us when things got bad.

Clearly I first saw you smilin' in the sun.

I wanna feel your warmth upon me. I wanna be the one.

I will remember you.

Will you remember me?

Don't let your life pass you by.

Weep not for the memories.

I'm so tired that I can't sleep.

Standin' on the edge of somethin' much too deep.

It's funny how we feel so much but cannot say a word.

We are screaming inside, oh, we can't be heard.

I will remember you.

Will you remember me?

Don't let your life pass you by.

Weep not for the memories.

So afraid to love you, more afraid to lose.

Clingin' to a past that doesn't let me choose.

Where once there was a darkness, a deep and endless night,

You gave me ev'rything you had, oh, you gave me life.

And I will remember you.

Will you remember me?

Don't let your life pass you by.

Weep not for the memories.

And I will remember you.

Will you remember me?

Don't let your life pass you by.

Weep not for the memories.

Weep not for the memories.

I WILL REMEMBER YOU

Words and Music by Sarah McLachlan,
Seamus Egan and Dave Merenda

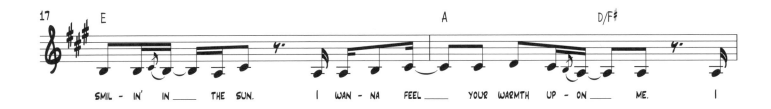

SMIL - IN' IN ___ THE SUN. I WAN - NA FEEL ___ YOUR WARMTH UP - ON ___ ME. I

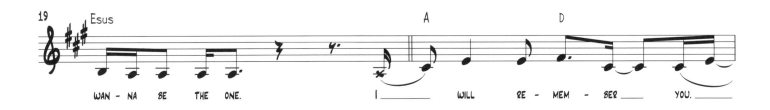

WAN - NA BE THE ONE. I ___ WILL RE - MEM - BER ___ YOU. ___

WILL YOU RE - MEM - BER ___ ME? ___ DON'T

LET YOUR LIFE ___ PASS ___ YOU BY. ___

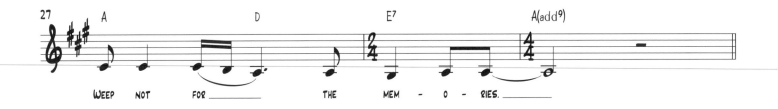

WEEP NOT FOR ___ THE MEM - O - RIES. ___

I'M ___ SO ___ TIRED ___ THAT I CAN'T SLEEP.

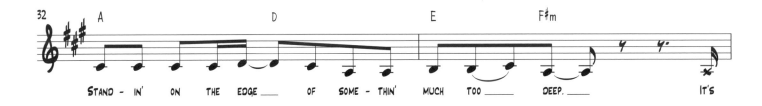

STAND - IN' ON THE EDGE ___ OF SOME - THIN' MUCH TOO ___ DEEP. ___ IT'S

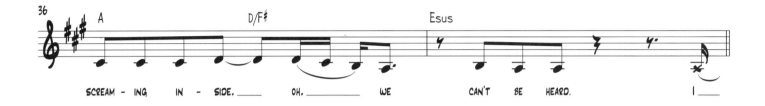

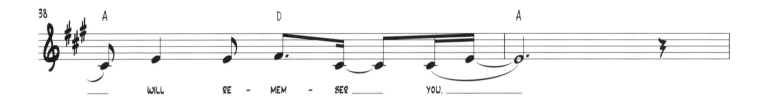

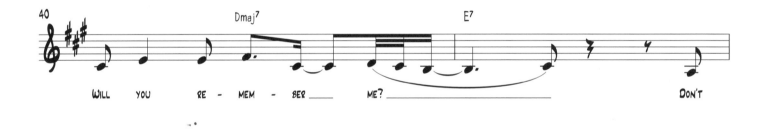

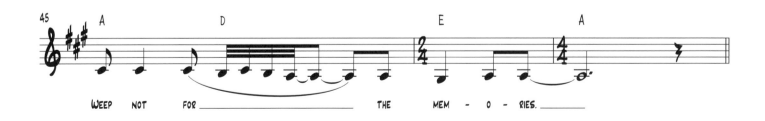

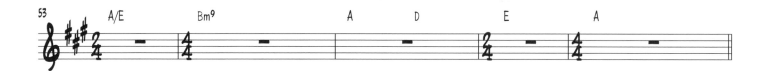

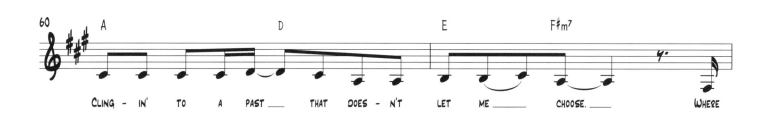

So a-fraid ___ to love ___ you. More a-fraid ___ to lose. ___

Cling - in' to a past ___ that does - n't let me ___ choose. ___ Where

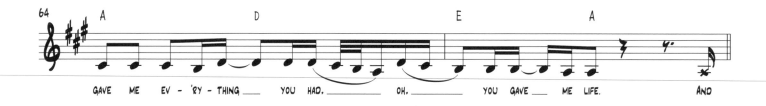

Once there was a dark - ness. ___ A deep and end - less night. ___ You

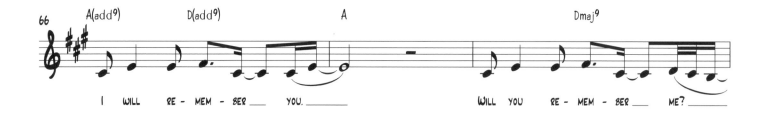

Gave me ev - 'ry-thing ___ you had. ___ Oh. ___ You gave ___ me life. And

I will re - mem - ber ___ you. ___ Will you re - mem - ber ___ me? ___

Don't let your life _____ pass ___ you by. ___

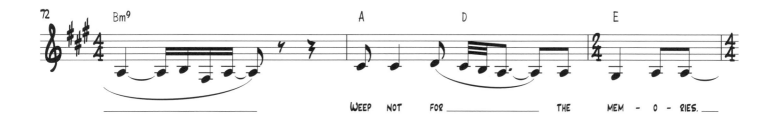

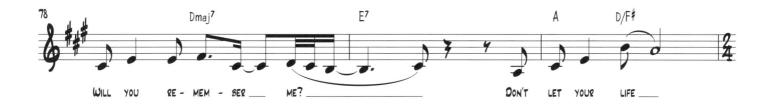

DANCING QUEEN

FUN FACTS:

The demo (demonstration recording) for "Dancing Queen" was originally titled "Boogaloo" and included this second verse, which was ultimately replaced: "Baby, baby, you're out of sight / hey, you're looking all right tonight / when you come to the party / listen to the guys / they've got that look in their eyes."

PERFORMANCE TIPS: ▶

"Dancing Queen" has a very wide range which means it uses both the low "chest voice," the middle, and the high "head voice." To increase your range, practice the exercise below.

The notes are staccato (short) so use your abdominal muscles.

EXERCISE 1:

More songs like this can be found in *Mama Mia!* Pro Vocal Women's Edition, Volume 25 (HL00740367).

DANCING QUEEN

Words and Music by Benny Andersson,
Björn Ulvaeus and Stig Anderson

You can dance, you can jive,

Having the time of your life.

Ooh, see that girl, watch that scene,

Diggin' the dancing queen.

Friday night and the lights are low,

Looking out for a place to go.

Mm, where they play the right music, getting in the swing,

You come to look for a king.

Anybody could be that guy,

Night is young and the music's high;

With a bit of rock music ev'rything is fine.

You're in the mood for a dance,

And when you get the chance...

You are the dancing queen,

Young and sweet, only seventeen.

Dancing queen,

Feel the beat from the tambourine, oh yeah.

You can dance, you can jive,

Having the time of your life.

Ooh, see that girl, watch that scene,

Diggin' the dancing queen.

You're a teaser, you turn 'em on,

Leave them burning and then you're gone;

Looking out for another, anyone will do.

You're in the mood for a dance,

And when you get the chance...

You are the dancing queen,

Young and sweet, only seventeen.

Dancing queen,

Feel the beat from the tambourine, oh yeah.

You can dance, you can jive,

Having the time of your life.

Ooh, see that girl, watch that scene,

Diggin' the dancing queen.

Diggin' the dancing queen.

Dancing queen.

DANCING QUEEN

Words and Music by Benny Andersson,
Björn Ulvaeus and Stig Anderson